365 INSPIRATIONS
FOR A JOYFUL LIFE

WHITE STAR PUBLISHERS

365 INSPIRATIONS
FOR A JOYFUL LIFE

CONTENTS

OBJECTIVE: WELL-BEING

OBJECTIVE:

Is there a secret to "live well", in short to gaining deep, lasting, and satisfying well-being? Sometimes we only need good motivation to face a day full of commitments and difficulties. It is certainly difficult to learn not to be discouraged and to regard challenges with a proactive spirit of initiative, but also books like this one can come to your aid. It presents an approach that, starting from the linguistic dimension of well-being (as we find, for example, in the French and Italian languages, where bien-être *and* benessere *also show lexically the indissoluble link between the two concepts), aims to give new meaning to the dimension of "being" compared to the superficial one of "having". Well-being thus becomes the watchword for a lifestyle which no longer aims at the accumulation of material goods, that also, above all, aims at giving value to nonmaterial things - perhaps, for this reason, still more precious - like health, internal peace, the balanced relationship with others and the natural environment, enjoying each moment serenely, the joy of doing and of experimenting.*

The aphorisms, the maxims, the suggestions of authoritative figures, or simply the advice deriving from calm common sense or applicable to the practicality of daily life, which accompany the splendid, suggestive images in this book, have precisely this aim: to remind us, through meditation on some key elements in the search for true well-being, that life

WELL-BEING

is worth living through giving value to what we are, not only by calculating what we have. We can take advantage of the recovery of psychophysical balance to gain motivation to look to the future joyfully, and finally to become able to savor life in all its many facets. "Live, travel, adventure, bless, and don't be sorry," Jack Kerouac advised, placing the experience - the "doing" openly and joyously - in the center of the human being's existence.

The theme running through this book is thus the ability to find ourselves again and appreciate ourselves through a greater attention to the foundations of the quality of life. Above all, health, because physical well-being is the foundation of the entire architecture of a happy life. When Gandhi, for example, states that "It is health that is real wealth and not pieces of gold and silver" or Vergil tells us that "heath is the greatest form of wealth," they express with disarming simplicity what many, crushed by the inexorable mechanisms of the race for material success, sooner or later have to learn through hard experience. Stress, tiredness, a life filled with rushing about but also paradoxically sedentary, and hurried and unhealthy (or even harmful) eating inevitably affect the psychophysical equilibrium of the organism, which is the guarantee of good health. As well as the affirmation of the great principles of life, we also find, on page after page, advice on the right diet, on natural *supplements, on exercises for the body and for posture, on the optimization of sleep, and still others intended to ensure (or ensure once again), one step at a time, the good health of the organism, the foundation of an excellent quality of life.*

It is a real change of model, of care and of respect for ourselves. Obviously, no one can expect it to be immediate and radical. What emerges from the suggestions in the book - which are not prescriptive, but aim to persuade us to think - is rather the idea of progressive improvement in our lifestyle and new and higher principles, which are capable in time of turning the tide: a similar concept to the one well known to industrial quality managers, of "continuous improvement", the only guarantee of always succeeding in doing things well.

Good physical health, psychological equilibrium, and serenity go hand in hand. Gandhi, again, warned us of the importance of "positive thinking": facing life with a positive spirit means rooting in our behavior habits and values which will become our mode of life (our "destiny", in the words of the wise Indian), taking control for ourselves of our existence and looking with renewed hope to a future which we feel to be in our hands. "I believe that if one always looked at the skies, one would end up with wings," are the words of Gustave Flaubert, which distill very well this attitude of confidence in our inner strength.

Thus, not meekly following abstract principles, but strong motivation - also in the sense of healthy competition with ourselves - to progressively achieve the objectives which open the door to true happiness (perhaps allowing ourselves, now and then, to break the rules a little, to add a little spice to a happy life), and offer the tools to build a future without the bitterness deriving from drifting with the tide.

We are protagonists in a change enabling us to build interactions with others on new foundations, through a new self-confidence replacing assertiveness with listening, competition with empathy, and subordination with equal relationships. The relationships that are established thus become an opportunity for exchanging experiences and a further source of inner richness... without forgetting a healthy dose of carefree lightness, the only real weapon to tackle difficulties: "Let your life lightly dance on the edges of Time like dew on the tip of a leaf," the Indian poet and philosopher, Rabindranath Tagore, reminds us opportunely in a wish for radiant happiness.

With its fascinating and evocative images, this book is thus a stimulus to reflection both on the great themes of existence and on the choices that in everyday life can make the difference and open the way toward a happy life rich in real fulfillment. A bedside book that, page after page, reminds us that we are human beings, not machines.

1

January

Keep your thoughts positive,
because your thoughts become your words.
Keep your words positive,
because your words become your behavior.
Keep your behavior positive,
because your behavior become your habits.
Keep your habits positive,
because your habits become your values.
Keep your values positive,
because your values become your destiny.

– Mahatma Gandhi

JANUARY

2

January

Life is like a tree and its root is
consciousness. Therefore, once we
tend the root, the tree as a whole
will be healthy.

– Deepak Chopra

3

January

Water, air, and cleanliness are
the chief articles in my pharmacopoeia.

– Napoleon I

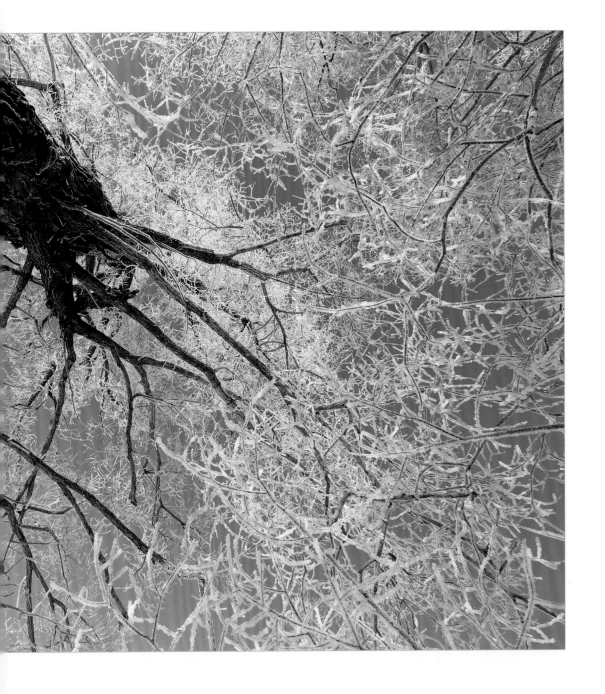

4

January

Look wide, and even when you think
you are looking wide – look wider still.

– Robert Baden-Powell

5

January

True enjoyment comes from activity
of the mind and exercise of the body;
the two are ever united.

– Wilhelm von Humboldt

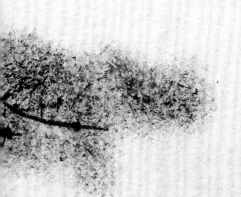

6

January

An answer is always on the stretch
of road that is behind you. Only a
question can point the way forward.

– *Jostein Gaarder*

7

January

Live, travel, adventure, bless
and don't be sorry.

– *Jack Kerouac*

8

January

Health is a state of complete
harmony of the body, mind and spirit.
When one is free from physical
disabilities and mental distractions,
the gates of the soul open.

– B.K.S. Iyengar

9

January

Look up at the stars and not down at
your feet. Try to make sense of what
you see, and wonder about what makes
the universe exist. Be curious.

– Stephen Hawking

10

January

How to reach a goal? Without haste but
without pause.

– Johann Wolfgang von Goethe

11

January

The effort without perseverance is a
waste of energy.

– T.Y.S. Lama Gangchen

12

January

A mind free from all disturbances is Yoga.

– Patanjali

13

January

Diseases of the soul are more dangerous and
more numerous than those of the body.

– Cicero

14

January

He who knows others is wise.
He who knows himself is enlightened.

– Lao Tzu

15

January

Face the facts of being what you are,
for that is what changes what you are.

– Søren Kierkegaard

16
January

Look deep into nature, and then you will
understand everything better.

– Albert Einstein

17
January

Be faithful in small things because
it is in them that your strength lies.

– Mother Theresa

18

January

Take care of your body. It's the only
place you have to live.

– Jim Rohn

19

January

Health is a state of complete physical,
mental and social well-being
and not merely the absence of disease
or infirmity.

– World Health Organization, 1948

20

January

A winner always finds a way,
a loser always finds an excuse.

– Lao Tzu

21

January

Your vision will become clear only
when you can look into your own heart.
He who looks outside, dreams.
He who looks inside, awakes.

– Carl Gustav Jung

22

January

Drink a cold glass of water with freshly
squeezed lemon every morning.
It hydrates, gives a dose of vitamin C,
boosts the immune system, and has
fat-burning benefits.

– Advice for your well-being

23

January

The two greatest misfortunes in life are
bad health and a bad conscience.

– Leo Tolstoy

24

January

He who has health has hope and
he who has hope has everything.

– Arabian Proverb

25

January

It takes considerable knowledge
just to realize the extent of your
own ignorance.

– Thomas Sowell

26

January

We are going to the moon –
that is not very far. Man has so much
farther to go within himself.

– Anaïs Nin

27

January

Man needs difficulties;
they are necessary for health.

– Carl Gustav Jung

28

January

It does not matter how slowly you go
as long as you do not stop.

– Confucius

29

January

Never allow waiting
to become a habit.
Live your dreams and take risks.
Life is happening now.

– Paulo Coelho

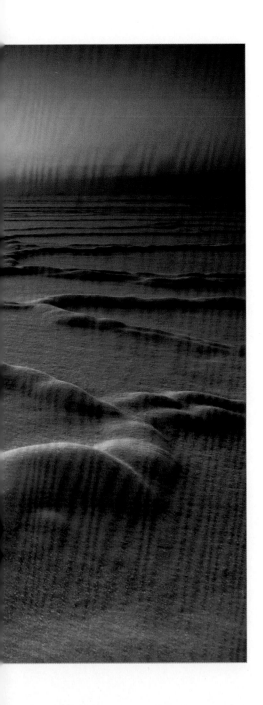

30

January

We may encounter many defeats but
we must not be defeated.

– Maya Angelou

31

January

You cannot travel the path until
you have become the path itself.

– Buddha

1

February

Just imagine becoming the way you used
to be as a very young child,
before you understood the meaning of any word,
before opinions took over your mind.
The real you is loving, joyful, and free.
The real you is just like a flower,
just like the wind,
just like the ocean,
just like the sun.

– Don Miguel Ruiz

FEBRUARY

2

February

Pursue some path, however narrow and crooked,
in which you can walk with love and reverence.

– Henry David Thoreau

3

February

One should not prize living as such,
but living well.

– Plato

4

February

To see things in the seed,
that is genius.

– Lao Tzu

5

February

Notice that the stiffest tree is most easily
cracked, while the bamboo or willow
survives by bending with the wind.

– Bruce Lee

6

February

Every day we should hear at least one
little song, read one good poem, see one
exquisite picture, and, if possible,
speak a few sensible words.

– Johann Wolfgang von Goethe

7

February

Riches are not from abundance
of worldly goods, but from
a contented mind.

– Muhammad

8

February

The part can never be well unless
the whole is well.

– Plato

9

February

Thirst is not a very good indicator of your level of hydration. By the time you feel thirsty, you're probably already getting dehydrated.

– Advice for your well-being

10

February

Balance itself is the good.

– Haruki Murakami

11

February

Today is your day to start fresh,
to eat right, to train hard, to live
healthy, to be proud.

– Advice for your well-being

12

February

For happy health, fuel yourself
with dreams and greens.

– Terri Guillemets

13

February

Health is like money:
we never have a true idea
of its value until we lose it.

– Josh Billings

14
February

There are two blessings which most people waste and whose value they do not appreciate: health and free time.

– Muhammad

15
February

Taking joy in living is a woman's best cosmetic.

– Rosalind Russell

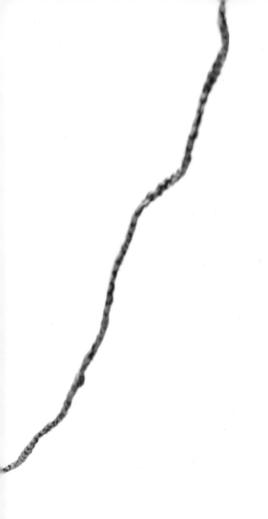

16
February

Live your beliefs and you can turn
the world around.

– Henry David Thoreau

17
February

Life would be tragic
if it weren't funny.

– Stephen Hawking

18

February

Give light, and the darkness
will disappear of itself.

– Desiderius Erasmus

19

February

Keep inside you a little fire burning;
however small, however hidden.

– Cormac McCarthy

20

February

This life that has been given to us as a gift, as such
a precious gift. To really try to understand it, really
try to recognize it, is the greatest meditation.
Through the media of this knowledge we can tap
into our inner sources that are so beautiful.

– Prem Rawat

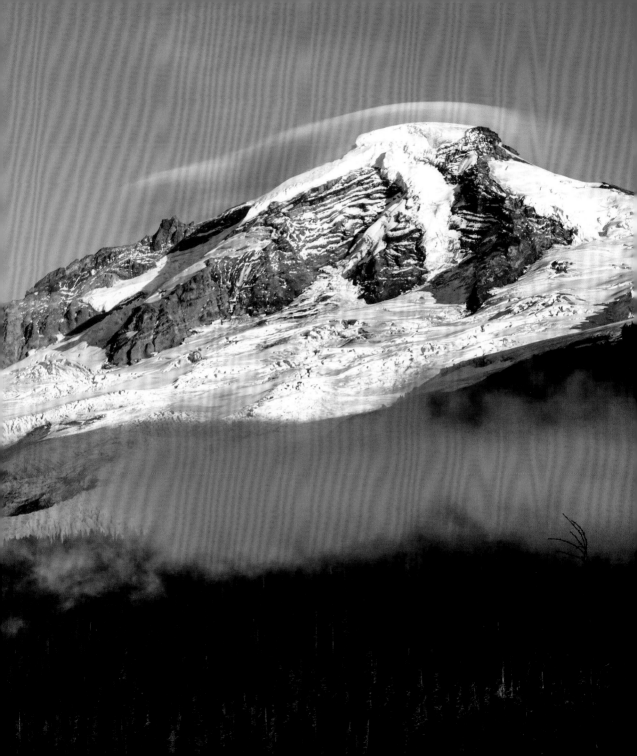

21

February

Two quite opposite qualities equally
affect our minds - habits and novelty.

– Jean de La Bruyère

22

February

If today I go to bed not having done
something new compared to yesterday,
then a day has been wasted.

– Bill Gates

23
February

Cook with spices and herbs:
antioxidant-rich herbs and spices
can block the formation of harmful
compounds that are associated with
aging and may inhibit tissue damage
caused by high levels of blood sugar.

– Advice for your well-being

24
February

To avoid sickness eat less;
to prolong life worry less.

– Chu Hui Weng

25
February

To keep the body in good health is a
duty, otherwise we shall not be able to
keep our mind strong and clear.

– Buddha

26
February

Ease tension migraine by massaging
the temples with peppermint oil,
tiger balm or white flower oil.

– Advice for your well-being

27
February

Our greatest weakness lies in giving up.
The most certain way to succeed is
always to try just one more time.

– Thomas A. Edison

28/29
February

We do not need magic to change the
world, we carry all the power we need
inside ourselves already: we have the
power to imagine better.

– Joanne Kathleen Rowling

1
March

Let your life lightly dance on the edges
of time like dew on the tip of a leaf.

– Rabindranath Tagore

MARCH

2

March

Try to be a rainbow in someone's cloud.

– Maya Angelou

3

March

What makes the desert beautiful is that somewhere it hides a well.

– Antoine de Saint-Exupéry

4

March

The purpose of meditation is personal transformation.

– Henepola Gunaratana

5

March

How wonderful it is that nobody need wait a single moment
before starting to improve the world.

– Anne Frank

6

March

From a small seed a mighty trunk may grow.

– Aeschylus

7

March

Start by doing what's necessary;
then do what's possible;
and suddenly you are doing the impossible.

– Francis of Assisi

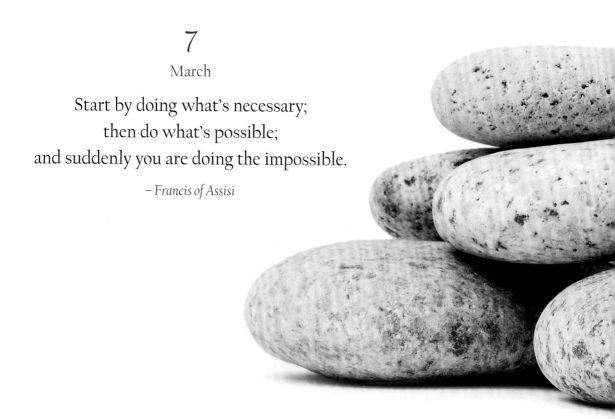

8

March

The future belongs to those who believe
in the beauty of their dreams.

– Eleanor Roosevelt

9

March

I believe that if one always looked
at the skies, one would end up
with wings.

– Gustave Flaubert

10
March

They will tell you that you aren't enough. Do not be fooled, you are much better than they want you to believe you are.

– Pope John Paul II

11
March

The free soul is rare, but you know it when you see it – basically because you feel good when you are near or with them.

– Charles Bukowski

12
March

Lack of activity destroys the good condition of every human being, while movement and methodical physical exercise save it and preserve it.

– Plato

13
March

Smile, breathe, and go slowly.

– *Thich Nhat Hanh*

14
March

Laugh when you can, apologize when you should and let go of what you can't change.

– *Stephen Hawking*

15
March

Time is a game played beautifully by children.

– *Heraclitus*

16

March

Meditation can help us embrace our
worries, our fear, our anger; and that is
very healing. We let our own natural
capacity of healing do the work.

– *Thich Nhat Hanh*

17

March

We are born weak, we need strength;
helpless, we need aid; foolish, we need reason.
All that we lack at birth, all that
we need when we come to man's estate,
is the gift of education.

– *Jean-Jacques Rousseau*

18
March

Life is not a problem to be solved,
but a reality to be experienced.

– *Søren Kierkegaard*

19
March

The energy of the mind
is the essence of life.

– *Aristotle*

20

March

Among the numerous therapeutic
properties of ginger, there is that
of reinvigorating the entire organism.
It has digestive and anti-inflammatory
qualities, and combats arthrosis
and the stress of daily life.

– Advice for your well-being

21

March

Tisanes based on hibiscus or
hibiscus tea, by means of their
powerful anti-oxidants, combat
cell damage and support the
immune system.

– Advice for your well-being

22

March

The purpose of meditation is to make
our mind calm and peaceful. If our mind
is peaceful, we will be free from worries
and mental discomfort, and so we will
experience true happiness.
But if our mind is not peaceful,
we will find it very difficult to be happy,
even if we are living in the very best conditions.

– Kelsang Gyatso

23

March

Two things contribute to progress: going
faster than the others or being on track.

– Descartes

24

March

Beauty is not in the face; beauty is a
light in the heart.

– Kahlil Gibran

25

March

I don't like standard beauty - there is no
beauty without strangeness.

– Karl Lagerfeld

26
March

There is a millenarian fresh water
deposit in my soul.

– Abdelmajid Benjelloun

27
March

Water is the power that tempers you,
you find yourself, renew
yourself in her...

– Eugenio Montale

28
March

Fear less, hope more; eat less, chew more;
whine less, breathe more; talk less, say more;
hate less, love more; and all good
things are yours.

– Swedish Proverb

29
March

To sleep better go to bed at the same time
every night and get up at the same time every
morning – even on weekends. A regular sleep
routine keeps your biological clock steady so
you rest better.

– Advice for your well-being

30

March

Usage hides the true aspect
of things from us.

– *Michel de Montaigne*

31

March

Take the course opposite to custom
and you will almost always do well.

– *Jean-Jacques Rousseau*

1

April

Our time here is magic!
It's the only space you have
to realize whatever it is that is beautiful,
whatever is true,
whatever is great, whatever is potential,
whatever is rare,
whatever is unique, in.
It's the only space.

– Ben Okri

APRIL

2

April

A child can teach an adult three things:
1. To be happy for no reason.
2. To always be busy with something.
3. To know how to demand with all his
might that which he desires.

– Paulo Coelho

3

April

Don't forget to love yourself.

– Søren Kierkegaard

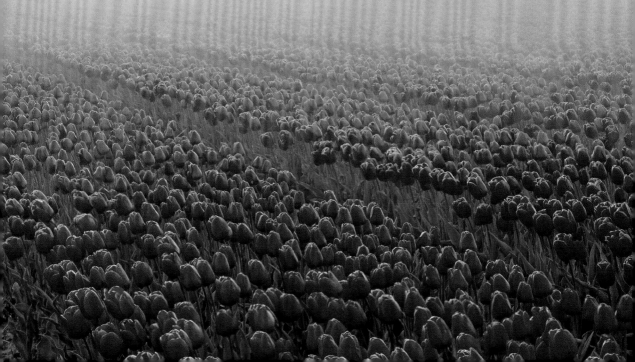

4

April

To forget how to dig the earth and
to tend the soil is to forget ourselves.

– *Mahatma Gandhi*

5

April

Do not look upon this world
with fear and loathing.
Bravely face whatever the gods offer.

– *Morihei Ueshiba*

6

April

We are all part of creation, all kings,
all poets, all musicians; we have only
to open up, only to discover what is
already there.

– *Henry Miller*

7

April

What you do today can improve all
your tomorrows.

– *Ralph Marston*

8

April

Health is the greatest gift, contentment
the greatest wealth, faithfulness
the best relationship.

– *Buddha*

9

April

Drink fluids at regular intervals
during the day.

10

April

Iron works to deliver oxygen to the
body and to keep your immune system
healthy. Iron can be found in oatmeal,
lentils, kidney beans, leafy greens,
red meat, poultry, fish, whole grains,
dried fruit.

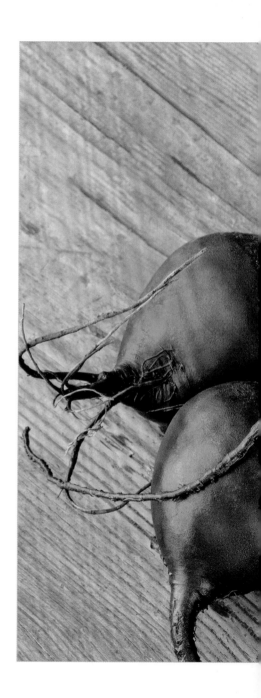

11

April

A good laugh and a long sleep are the two best cures for anything.

– Irish proverb

12

April

God bless the inventor of sleep, the cloak that covers all men's thoughts.

– Miguel de Cervantes

13
April

Your heart is full of fertile seeds,
waiting to sprout.

– Morihei Ueshiba

14
April

Well done is better than well said.

– Benjamin Franklin

15
April

It does not matter how slowly you go
as long as you do not stop.

– Confucius

16
April

Spread love everywhere you go.
Let no one ever come to you
without leaving happier.

– Mother Theresa

17
April

We know what we are,
but know not what we may be.

– William Shakespeare

18

April

Turn down the thermostat: 55-59°F
(15-18°C) is the best temp for restful
sleep. A cool bedroom helps promote
the drop in core body temperature
necessary to induce sleep.

– Advice for your well-being

19

April

It is better to light a candle
than to curse the darkness.

– Lao Tzu

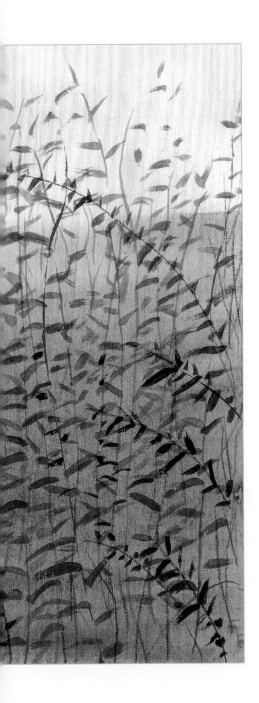

20
April

Who seeks shall find.

– Sophocles

21
April

Intelligence is the ability
to adapt to change.

– Stephen Hawking

22
April

In all things of nature there is
something of the marvelous.

– Aristotle

23
April

Do the difficult things while they are easy and do the great things while they are small. A journey of a thousand miles must begin with a single step.

– Lao Tzu

24
April

An early-morning walk is a blessing for the whole day.

– Henry David Thoreau

25

April

You can't cross the sea merely by standing and staring at the water.

– Rabindranath Tagore

26

April

Challenges are what make life interesting; overcoming
them is what makes life meaningful.

– Joshua J. Marine

27
April

The only real insurance you have against disease is a healthy body. Invest wisely, generously and often in that policy.

– Advice for your well-being

28
April

Holy Basil: combat stress. The plant you use in your pesto sauce reduces stress by increasing adrenaline and noradrenaline and decreasing serotonin.

– Advice for your well-being

29
April

A disciplined mind
is valuable ally.

– from "Dhammapada"

30
April

There are moments of existence when time and space are more profound, and the awareness of existence is immensely heightened.

– Charles Baudelaire

1

May

Our bodies are our gardens –
our wills are our gardeners.

– William Shakespeare

MAY

2

May

A man is a success if he gets up
in the morning and gets to bed at night,
and in between he does what
he wants to do.

– Bob Dylan

3

May

A one hour workout is 4% of your day:
no excuses.

– Advice for your well-being

4

May

We are not going in circles, we are going
upwards. The path is a spiral; we have
already climbed many steps.

– Hermann Hesse

5

May

The cells in your body react to everything
that your mind says. Negativity brings
down your immune system.

– Advice for your well-being

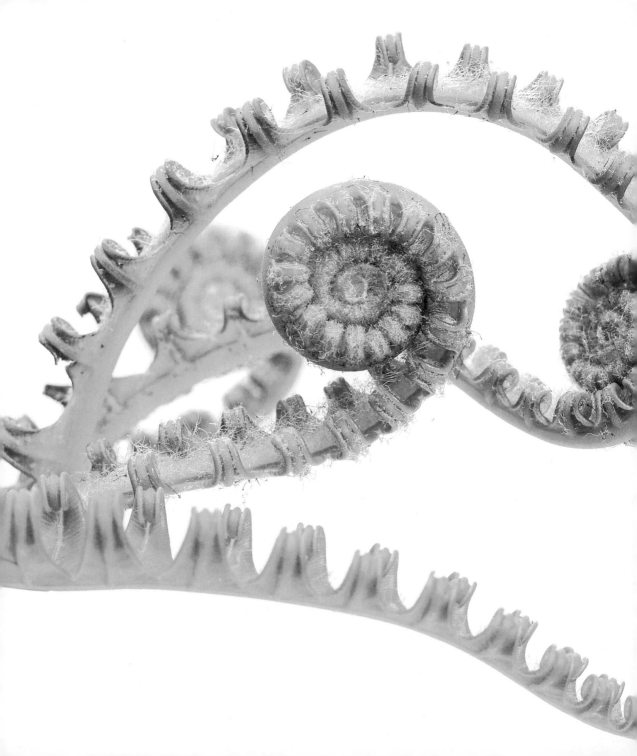

6
May

If you are never alone,
you cannot know yourself.

– Paulo Coelho

7
May

Meditation is to dive all the way
within, beyond thought, to the source
of thought and pure consciousness.
It enlarges the container, every time you
transcend. When you come out, you
come out refreshed, filled with energy
and enthusiasm for life.

– David Lynch

8
May

I know where I'm going and
I know the truth, and I don't have
to be what you want me to be.
I'm free to be what I want.

– Muhammad Ali

9
May

Read your fate, see what is before you,
and walk on into futurity.

– Henry David Thoreau

10

May

Life is growth. If we stop growing,
technically and spiritually,
we are as good as dead.

– Morihei Ueshiba

11

May

Transform all your energy into
an opportunity to live a happy life.
Take the right road, that of your values.

– Stephen Littleword

12

May

Many of life's failures are people who
did not realize how close they were to
success when they gave up.

– Thomas A. Edison

13

May

If we did all the things
we are capable of, we would literally
astound ourselves.

– Thomas A. Edison

14

May

It's fine to celebrate success
but it is more important
to heed the lessons of failure.

– Bill Gates

15

May

The groundwork for all happiness
is good health.

– Leigh Hunt

16

May

The fewer comforts one has and the fewer
needs one has. The fewer needs one has,
the happier one is.

– Jules Verne

17

May

It is health that is the real wealth and not
pieces of gold and silver.

– Mahatma Gandhi

18

May

Drink green tea: its catechins,
antioxidants, and caffeine help increase
the metabolic generation of heat. Drink
a cup about 10 minutes before exercising.

– Advice for your well-being

19

May

The patient man makes
his own happiness.

– Publilius Syrus

20

May

Running is the open space where
thoughts come to play.

– Mark Rowlands

21
May

Eat clean. Think straight.
Work consistently. Speak positively.
Motivate others. Believe in yourself.

– Advice for your well-being

22
May

Modern psychology has pointed to the need of
educating people to use a much larger portion of
the mind. Transcendental meditation fulfills this
need. And it can be taught very easily.

– Maharishi Mahesh Yogi

23
May

Nothing contributes less to serenity than wealth,
and nothing contributes more than health.

– Arthur Schopenhauer

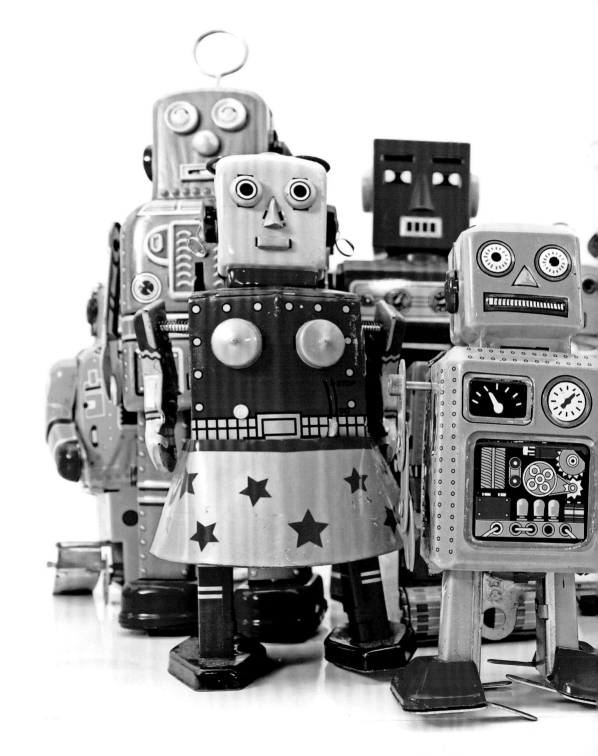

24
May

The greatest pleasure of doing
something lies in the thought
of being able to tell a friend.

– Linda MacFarlane

25
May

Only knowing me, knowing my inner self,
can I speak to the interiority of others.

– Susanna Tamaro

26
May

In nature, light creates color; in the
picture, color creates light.

– Hans Hofmann

27
May

Life is a great big canvas; throw
all the paint you can at it.

– Danny Kaye

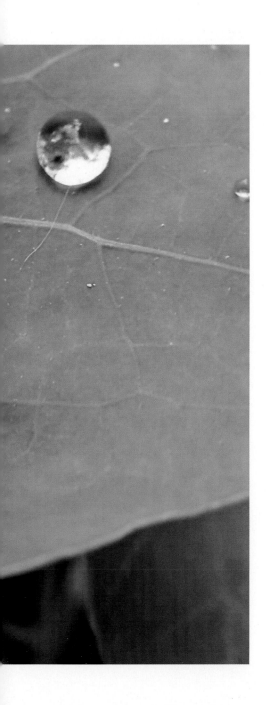

28
May

The only source of knowledge
is experience.

– Albert Einstein

29
May

Vitality shows in not only the ability to
persist but the ability to start over.

– F. Scott Fitzgerald

30

May

Meditation makes the entire nervous system
go into a field of coherence.

– Deepak Chopra

31

May

Physical fitness is not only one of the most
important keys to a healthy body, it is the basis
of dynamic and creative intellectual activity.

– John F. Kennedy

1

June

Regularity in the hours of rising and retiring,
perseverance in exercise,
adaptation of dress to the variations of climate,
simple and nutritious aliment,
and temperance in all things
are necessary branches of the regimen of health.

– Philip Stanhope, 4th Earl of Chesterfield

JUNE

2

June

What a paternity that of trees, which
can give to each of their branches a path
towards the light.

– Lorenzo Oliván

3

June

Meditation is painful in the beginning
but it bestows immortal bliss and
supreme joy in the end.

– Swami Sivananda

4

June

The greatest wealth is health.

– Virgil

5

June

Blueberries have some of the highest levels of an antioxidant known as anthocyanin, and they've been linked to all kinds of positive health outcomes, including sharper cognition.

– Advice for your well-being

6

June

To be truly balanced and serene, it is indispensable that one does what one really wants, and not what others want.

– Lorenzo Licalzi

7

June

The highest and most beautiful things in life
are not to be heard about, nor read about,
nor seen but, if one will, are to be lived.

– Søren Kierkegaard

8

June

St. John's wort not only contains melatonin,
the hormone that regulates our sleep-wake
cycles, but it also increases the body's own
melatonin, improving sleep.

– Advice for your well-being

9
June

Imperfection is beauty, madness is genius and it's better to be absolutely ridiculous than absolutely boring.

– Marilyn Monroe

10
June

To be prepared is half the victory.

– Miguel de Cervantes

11

June

He who knows that enough is enough will always have enough.

– Lao Tzu

12

June

If I can see it and believe it, then I can achieve it.

– Arnold Schwarzenegger

13

June

Water is a healthy choice for hydration,
without adding calories to your diet.

– Advice for your well-being

14

June

All parts of the body which have a function,
if used in moderation and exercised in labors
in which each is accustomed, become thereby
healthy, well developed and age more slowly,
but if unused they become liable to disease,
defective in growth and age quickly.

– Hippocrates

15

June

Health is the first duty in life.

– Oscar Wilde

16

June

What lies behind us and what lies ahead
of us are tiny matters compared
to what lives within us.

– Henry David Thoreau

17

June

Give every day the chance to become
the most beautiful day of your life.

– Mark Twain

18

June

To combat stress, take a hot bath and add
a few drops of essential oil of lavender.

– Advice for your well-being

19

June

The key to growth is the introduction
of higher dimensions of consciousness
into our awareness.

– Lao Tzu

20

June

In a disordered mind, as in a disordered body, soundness of health is impossible.

– Cicero

21

June

The two most important things in this world are health and time; the trick is to take advantage of the first when you still have the second.

– Charles Edouard de Valhubert

22
June

The young man walks faster than the older, but the older knows the way.

– African Proverb

23
June

Probable impossibilities are to be preferred to improbable possibilities.

– Aristotle

24

June

If every day you practice walking and
sitting meditation and generate the
energy of mindfulness and concentration
and peace, you are a cell in the body of
the new Buddha. This is not a dream but
is possible today and tomorrow.

– Thich Nhat Hanh

25
June

Life finds its purpose and fulfillment
in the expansion of happiness.

– Maharishi Mahesh Yogi

26
June

Discipline is the bridge between goals
and accomplishment.

– Jim Rohn

27
June

Wherever you go, go with
all your heart.

– *Confucius*

28
June

The heart of a human being is no
different from the soul of heaven and
earth. In your practice always keep in
your thoughts the interaction of heaven
and earth, water and fire, yin and yang.

– *Morihei Ueshiba*

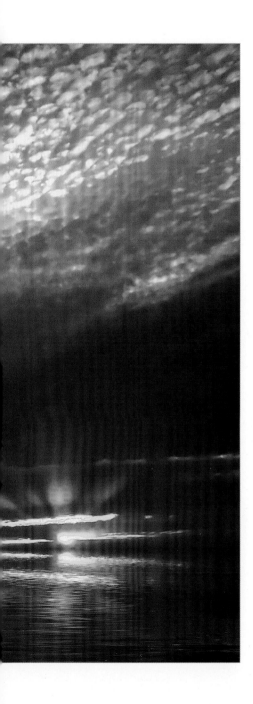

29

June

Each man should look inside himself
to learn the meaning of life. It is not
something discovered: it is something
that must be molded.

– Antoine de Saint-Exupéry

30

June

We become just by performing just
action, temperate by performing
temperate actions, brave by performing
brave action.

– Aristotle

1

July

Eating is not merely a material pleasure.
Eating well gives a spectacular joy to life and
contributes immensely to goodwill and happy companionship.
It is of great importance to the morale.

– Elsa Schiaparelli

JULY

2

July

Conscience is a muscle that must be trained and, as for the athlete, the exercise requires a certain discipline.

– Beppe Severgnini

3

July

Life is being a versatile athlete and training oneself in every field of life.

– Ray Anthony Lewis

4

July

If you don't like something, change it.
If you can't change it, change your attitude.

– Maya Angelou

5

July

You must live in the present, launch yourself on every wave,
find your eternity in each moment.

– Henry David Thoreau

6

July

Health is a relationship between you
and your body.

– Terri Guillemets

7

July

Movement is the best cure for melancholy.

– Bruce Chatwin

8

July

If you don't design your own life plan, chances are
you'll fall into someone else's plan. And guess what
they have planned for you? Not much.

– Jim Rohn

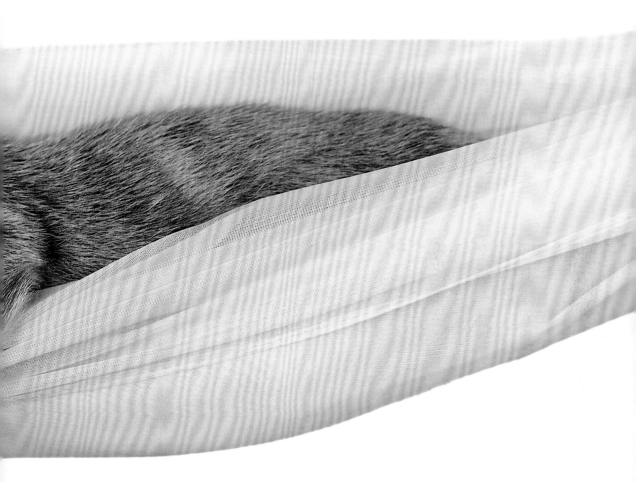

9

July

What man is happy? He who has a healthy body,
a resourceful mind, and a docile nature.

– *Thales of Miletus*

10
July

I met the sea meditating on a drop of dew.

– Kahlil Gibran

11
July

The cure of the part should not be attempted
without the cure of the whole.

– Plato

12

July

Sniff rosemary: catching a whiff of this
aromatic herb may increase alertness
and improve memory.

– Advice for your well-being

13

July

Use herbal remedy!
Sage can relieve a sore throat.

– Advice for your well-being

14

July

Strawberries, raspberries, and blackberries, are rich in vitamin C, which has been shown to be helpful in combating stress.

– Advice for your well-being

15

July

Taking cinnamon extract daily successfully reduced blood sugar by about 10%.

– Advice for your well-being

16
July

Do the one thing you think you cannot do.
Fail at it. Try again. Do better the second
time. The only people who never tumble are
those who never mount the high wire.
This is your moment. Own it.

– Oprah Winfrey

17
July

Happiness is a state of inner fulfillment,
not the gratification of inexhaustible
desires for outward things.

– Matthieu Ricard

18

July

Don't move the way fear makes
you move. Move the way love
makes you move. Move the way joy
makes you move.

– Osho

19

July

Do you wish to rise? Begin by
descending. You plan a tower that
will pierce the clouds? Lay first the
foundation of humility.

– Saint Augustine

20

July

People need to know that they have all the
tools within themselves. Self-awareness,
which means awareness of their body,
awareness of their mental space, awareness of
their relationships – not only with each other,
but with life and the ecosystem.

– *Deepak Chopra*

21

July

Miracles are a retelling in small letters
of the very same story which is written
across the whole world in letters too
large for some of us to see.

– *C. S. Lewis*

22

July

They say that when a person looks up at the stars, it is as if he wanted to find again his dimension dispersed in the universe.

– Salvador Dalí

23
July

Put your heart, mind, and soul into
even your smallest acts.
This is the secret of success.

– Swami Sivananda

24
July

When there are thoughts, it is
distraction: when there are no
thoughts, it is meditation.

– Ramana Maharshi

25
July

Health is not valued until
sickness comes.

– Thomas Fuller

26

July

Good habits formed at youth
make all the difference.

– Aristotle

27

July

Body is not stiff, mind is stiff.

– Sri K. Pattabhi Jois

28

July

Yoga is the perfect opportunity to be curious
about who you are.

– Jason Crandell

29

July

Yoga is invigoration in relaxation.
Freedom in routine.
Confidence through self control.
Energy within and energy without.

– Ymber Delecto

30
July

Eat avocados: they're rich in monounsaturated fat and vitamin E, both of which promote healthy skin.

– Advice for your well-being

31
July

Turmeric ease arthritis. A heaping helping of curry could relieve your pain. That's because turmeric, a spice used in curry, contains curcumin, a powerful anti-inflammatory.

– Advice for your well-being

1

August

I know of no single formula for success. But over the years
I have observed that some attributes of leadership are universal and
are often about finding ways of encouraging people
to combine their efforts, their talents, their insights,
their enthusiasm and their inspiration to work together.

– Queen Elizabeth II

AUGUST

2

August

However difficult life may seem,
there is always something you can do
and succeed at.

– Stephen Hawking

3

August

The more intensely we feel about an
idea or a goal, the more assuredly the
idea, buried deep in our subconscious,
will direct us along the path to its
fulfillment.

– Earl Nightingale

4

August

Do your little bit of good where you are;
its those little bits of good put together
that overwhelm the world.

– Desmond Tutu

5

August

The ultimate value of life depends
upon awareness and the power
of contemplation rather than upon
mere survival.

– Aristotle

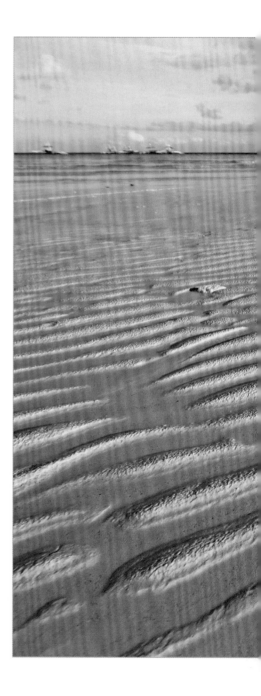

6

August

Whether you're keeping a journal or writing as a meditation, it's the same thing. What's important is you're having a relationship with your mind.

– Natalie Goldberg

7

August

Breathe deeply. For fast focus, sit in a comfortable place, breathe naturally, and settle your attention on your breath.

– Advice for your well-being

8

August

Meditation is the dissolution
of thoughts in eternal awareness
or pure consciousness without
objectification, knowing without
thinking, merging finitude
in infinity.

– *Voltaire*

9

August

People won't have time for you
if you are always angry
or complaining.

– *Stephen Hawking*

10

August

Press a spot on your face to relieve
tension. Find the base of each cheekbone
and press lightly for 30 seconds.

– Advice for your well-being

11

August

Rubbing your feet can work out any
tightness while encouraging blood flow
to the foot.

– Advice for your well-being

12

August

A man who as a physical being is always
turned toward the outside, thinking that
his happiness lies outside him, finally
turns inward and discovers that the
source is within him.

– Søren Kierkegaard

13

August

If you look into your own heart, and you
find nothing wrong there, what is there
to worry about? What is there to fear?

– Confucius

14

August

When you are content to be simply
yourself and don't compare or compete,
everybody will respect you.

– Lao Tzu

15

August

In a gentle way, you can shake
the world.

– Mahatma Gandhi

16
August

Dogs do not lie to you about how they feel because they cannot lie about feelings. Nobody has ever seen a sad dog pretending to be happy.

– Jeffrey Masson

17
August

As long as he has a dog, he has a friend; and the poorer he gets, the better friend he has.

– Will Rogers

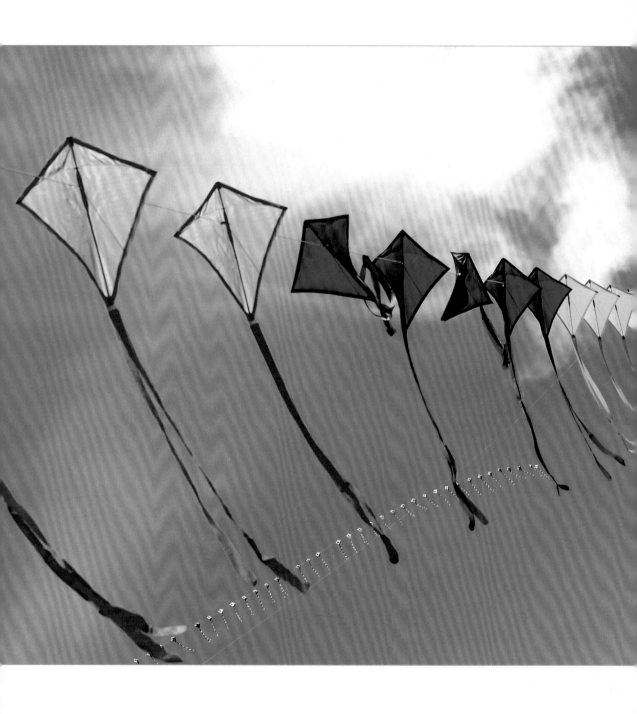

18
August

Mindfulness is a quality that's always there. It's an illusion that there's a meditation and post-meditation period, which I always find amusing, because you're either mindful or you're not.

– Richard Gere

19
August

Knowing is not enough;
we must apply.
Willing is not enough;
we must do.

– Johann Wolfgang von Goethe

20

August

Our greatest glory is not in never falling,
but in rising every time we fall.

– Confucius

21

August

He who is contented is rich.

– Lao Tzu

22

August

If we could give every individual the right amount of nourishment and exercise, not too little and not too much, we would have found the safest way to health.

– Hippocrates

23

August

Oatmeal causes your brain to produce serotonin, a feel-good chemical. Not only does serotonin have antioxidant properties, it also creates a soothing feeling that helps overcome stress.

– Advice for your well-being

24

August

Much effort, much prosperity.

– *Euripides*

25

August

Get action. Seize the moment. Man was never intended
to become an oyster.

– *Theodore Roosevelt*

26
August

Tactics, fitness, stroke ability,
adaptability, experience, and
sportsmanship are all necessary
for winning.

– Fred Perry

27
August

Success is a lousy teacher.
It seduces smart people into thinking
they can't lose.

– Bill Gates

28

August

It's not what you look at that matters,
it's what you see.

– Henry David Thoreau

29

August

You will find more lessons in the woods
than in books. The trees and rocks
will teach you what you will not learn
elsewhere.

– St. Bernard of Clairvaux

30
August

The gift of learning to meditate
is the greatest gift you can give
yourself in this lifetime.

– Sogyal Rinpoche

31
August

Yoga teaches us to cure what need
not be endured and endure
what cannot be cured.

– B.K.S. Iyengar

1

September

If there is magic on this planet,
it is contained in water.

– Loren Eiseley

SEPTEMBER

2

September

If you do not change direction, you may
end up where you are heading.

– Lao Tzu

3

September

The sun is never so beautiful as the day
we are on our way.

– Jean Giono

4

September

Don't judge each day by the harvest you
reap but by the seeds that
you plant.

– Robert Louis Stevenson

5

September

Happiness is not something you
postpone for the future; it is something
you design for the present.

– Jim Rohn

6
September

The will to win, the desire to succeed,
the urge to reach your full potential...
these are the keys that will unlock the
door to personal excellence.

– Confucius

7
September

He who conquers others is strong;
He who conquers himself is mighty.

– Lao Tzu

8

September

Serenity is to be at peace with
themselves and in harmony with others.

– Samuel Smiles

9

September

Take a bath in the evening. It helps to calm down,
fall asleep quickly and stay asleep through the night.

– Advice for your well-being

10

September

At the center of your being you have the
answer; you know who you are and you
know what you want.

– Lao Tzu

11

September

You can never get to know yourself
through contemplation, but only
through action.

– Johann Wolfgang von Goethe

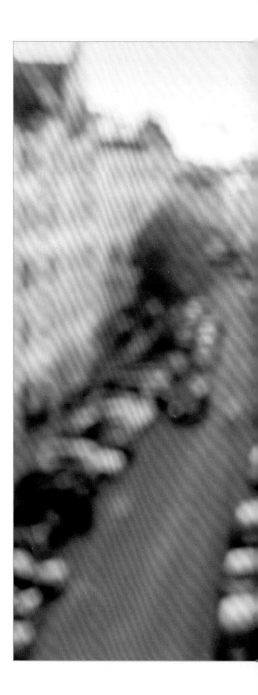

12

September

Remember that man does not live other life than the one he is lives at this time, nor loses any other life than the one that he loses now.

– Marcus Aurelius

13

September

If you are lucky enough to find a way of life you love, you have to find the courage to live it.

– John Irving

14

Ginger helps regulate blood flow, which may lower blood pressure,
and its anti-inflammatory properties might help ease arthritis.

– Advice for your well-being

15

September

Take chamomile: the flowers have been used for centuries as a gentle calmative for young and old alike.

– Advice for your well-being

16

September

Always laugh when you can,
it is cheap medicine

– Lord Byron

17

September

It's kind of fun to do the impossible.

– Walt Disney

18

September

You don't always get what you wish for,
you always get what you work for.

– *Stephen Hawking*

19

September

The true sign of intelligence is not
knowledge but imagination.

– *Albert Einstein*

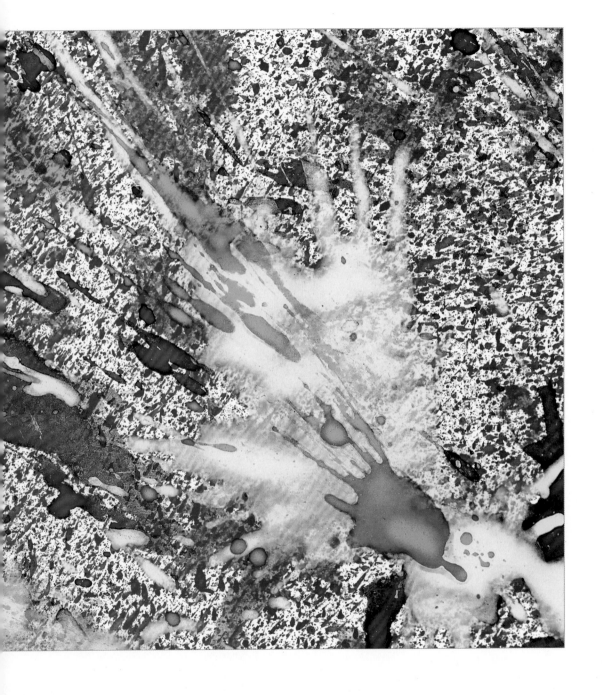

20
September

In the days of fog you can stop looking
for a moment, you can breathe, and
listen... close your eyes and concentrate
on your feelings, because even a foggy
day is not by accident.

– Stephen Littleword

21
September

The word "happiness" would lose
its meaning if it were not balanced
by sadness.

– Carl Gustav Jung

22

September

A human being with a settled purpose
must accomplish it, and nothing can
resist a will which will stake even
existence upon its fulfillment.

– Benjamin Disraeli

23

September

Nothing is so fatiguing as the eternal
hanging on of an uncompleted task.

– William James

24

September

Climbing is not necessary to conquer mountains; mountains remain motionless but we are no longer the same after that adventure.

– Royal Robbins

25

September

It is not enough to take steps which
may some day lead to a goal: each step
must be itself a goal and a step likewise.

– Johann Wolfgang von Goethe

26

September

Wealth I ask not, hope nor love,
nor a friend to know me;
all I ask, the heaven above
and the road below me.

– Robert Louis Stevenson

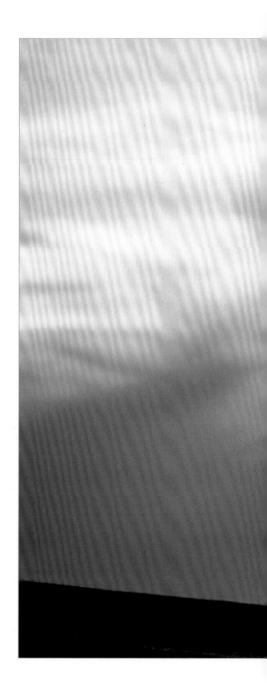

27

September

Don't walk behind me; I may not lead.
Don't walk in front of me;
I may not follow. Just walk beside me
and be my friend.

– Albert Camus

28

September

Being deeply loved by someone gives
you strength, while loving someone
deeply gives you courage.

– Lao Tzu

29
September

Count the flowers of your garden,
never falling leaves.

– *Romano Battaglia*

30
September

A sad soul can kill you quicker
than a germ.

– *John Steinbeck*

1

October

Positive thoughts (joy, happiness, fulfillment, achievement, worthiness) have positive results (enthusiasm, calm, well-being, ease, energy, love). Negative thoughts (judgment, unworthiness, mistrust, resentment, fear) produce negative results (tension, anxiety, alienation, anger, fatigue).

– Peter McWilliams

OCTOBER

2

October

The best way to predict your future
is to create it.

– Abraham Lincoln

3

October

He who learns but does not think, is
lost! He who thinks but does not learn
is in great danger.

– Confucius

4

October

Man is a genius when he is dreaming.

– Akira Kurosawa

5

October

The embrace is the highest language of
the soul and the body.

– Jacques de Bourbon

6
October

Being happy is of the utmost importance. Success in anything is through happiness.

– *Maharishi Mahesh Yogi*

7
October

Autumn is a second spring when every leaf is a flower.

– *Albert Camus*

8

October

Take advantage of morning air.

– Fryderyk Chopin

9

October

I love the rain, it washes memories off
the sidewalk of life.

– Woody Allen

10
October

Wrinkles should merely indicate
where smiles have been.

– *Mark Twain*

11
October

Each time a man laughs, he adds a
couple of days to his life.

– *Curzio Malaparte*

12

October

Meditation is not the construction of
something foreign, it is not an effort to
attain and then hold on to a particular
experience. We may have a secret
desire that through meditation
we will accumulate a stockpile of
magical experiences, or at least a
mystical trophy or two, and then
we will be able to proudly display
them for others to see.

– Sharon Salzberg

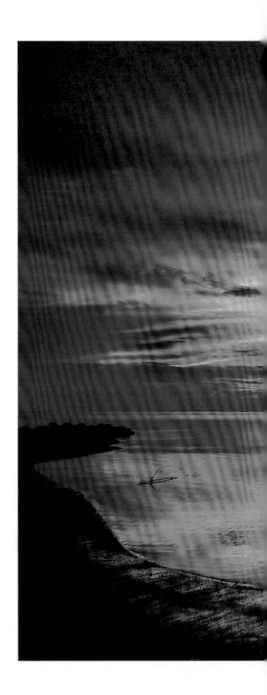

13

October

Even if I knew that tomorrow
the world would go to pieces,
I would still plant my apple tree.

– Martin Luther

14

October

He who takes medicine
and neglects to diet wastes
the skill of his doctors.

– Chinese Proverb

15

October

Be like the bamboo.
It is hard and compact outside, soft and hollow inside.
The roots are firmly planted in the ground
and intertwine with those of other plants
so that they strengthen and support each other.
The bamboo lets itself be blown by the wind but,
far from resisting it, it bends to it.
What bends is much more difficult to break.

– Buddhist thought

16

October

The rhythm of the body, the melody
of the mind, and the harmony
of the soul create the symphony of life.

– B. K. S. Iyengar

17

October

Peace comes from within.
Do not seek it without.

– Buddha

18

October

When you rise in the morning,
smile at your heart, your stomach,
your lungs, your liver.
After all, much depends
on them.

– Thich Nhat Hanh

19

October

Nothing is easier than self-deceit. For what each man wishes,
that he also believes to be true.

– Demosthenes

20

October

You will never do anything in this world without courage.
It is the greatest quality of the mind next to honor.

– Aristotle

21

October

Autumn is a wise season of good advice.

– Félix-Antoine Savard

22

October

The wise man does not lay up his own treasures.
The more he gives to others, the more he has for his own.

– Lao Tzu

23
October

Action is the foundational
key to all success.

– *Pablo Picasso*

24
October

Choosing a path meant having
to miss out on others. If one wants
to follow all possible paths,
one ends up following none.

– *Paulo Coelho*

25

October

Failure defeats loser,
failure inspires winners.

– Robert Kiyosaki

26

October

A healthy body is the guest-chamber of
the soul; a sick, its prison.

– Francis Bacon

27

October

Humility is the solid foundation
of all virtues.

– Confucius

28

October

Declining from the public ways, walk
in unfrequented paths.

– Pythagoras

29

October

A person who never made a mistake
never tried anything new.

– Albert Einstein

30
October

It is very important to know
who you are. To make decisions.
To show who you are.

– Malala Yousafzai

31
October

Wherever you go, no matter
what the weather, always bring
your own sunshine.

– Anthony J. D'Angelo

1
November

Find the time to reflect, it's the source of strength.
Find the time to play, it's the secret of youth.
Find the time to read, it's the foundacion of wisdom.
Find the time to be gentle, it's the road to happiness.
Find the time to dream, it's the path that carry you to the stars.
Find the time to love, it's the real joy of life.
Find the time to be happy, it's the music of the soul.

– Ancient Irish Ballad

NOVEMBER

2

November

Life is not merely to be alive,
but to be well.

– Marcus Valerius Martial

3

November

Never fear shadows. They simply
mean there's a light shining
somewhere nearby.

– Ruth E. Renkel

4

November

The best way to wake up your body
is through exercise. Exercise will get
your blood flowing and it makes you
feel more energized and provides
a rush of endorphins.

– Advice for your well-being

5

November

Crushed fresh garlic offers
the best cardiovascular
and cancer-fighting benefits.

– Advice for your well-being

6
November

Your body uses magnesium for a
number of critical activities, including
maintaining normal muscle and nerve
function, keeping heart rhythms steady,
helping regulate blood sugar levels...
You can find this mineral in pumpkin
seeds, spinach, and black beans.

– Advice for your well-being

7
November

The first recipe for happiness is:
avoid too lengthy meditation
on the past.

– André Maurois

8

November

Meditation is for everyone, and it's different for everyone. There is no right or wrong way of doing it, and meditation can help you increase your focus, reduce stress, and prevent common health ailments.

– Advice for your well-being

9

November

Wisdom, compassion, and courage are the three universally recognized moral qualities of men.

– Confucius

10
November

Happiness is not a matter
of intensity but of balance,
order, rhythm and harmony.

– *Thomas Merton*

11
November

A hidden harmony is better
than a visible.

– *Heraclitus*

12

November

Whatever you are, be a good one.

– Abraham Lincoln

13

November

In the middle of difficulty
lies opportunity.

– Albert Einstein

14

November

Well, when you're relaxed, your mind takes
you to the whole reality. There's no such thing
as time when you're really relaxed.
That's why meditation works.

– Shirley MacLaine

15

November

Some say that the rain is aimless
and others say it is full of memories
and desires.

– Tagor Manroo

16

November

Eat carrots, sweet potatoes, cantaloupe!
They all contain vitamin A,
the super nutrient which helps
maintain healthy vision,
boosts immune system functioning,
protects cognitive function.

– Advice for your well-being

17

November

The dried leaves and oil from the
eucalyptus tree contains chemicals that
may help control blood sugar levels,
support the immune system by fighting
bacteria and fungi, ease headache pain
and inflammation, decongest sinuses.

– Advice for your well-being

18

November

Perfection does not exist:
you can always do better
and you can always grow.

– Les Brown

19

November

Sit up straight! When you move from
poor posture to good posture, you
increase levels of energizing hormones,
as well as feel-good serotonin, plus you
decrease the stress hormone cortisol.

– Advice for your well-being

20
November

Never, never, never give up.

– Winston Churchill

21
November

Motivation is the art of getting people
to do what you want them to do
because they want to do it.

– Dwight D. Eisenhower

22
November

Total relaxation is the secret to
enjoying sitting meditation. I sit with
my spine upright, but not rigid; and
I relax all the muscles in my body.

– Thich Nhat Hanh

23
November

In meditation, leave the surface
to go deeply.
Become aware of a level of existence
below the frenetic activity of thoughts.

– Ulrich Ott

24

November

In oneself lies the whole world and if
you know how to look and learn, the
door is there and the key is in your hand.
Nobody on earth can give you either the
key or the door to open, except yourself.

– Jiddu Krishnamurti

25
November

We should feel sorrow, but not sink
under its oppression.

– Confucius

26
November

The purpose of training is to tighten up
the slack, toughen the body,
and polish the spirit.

– Morihei Ueshiba

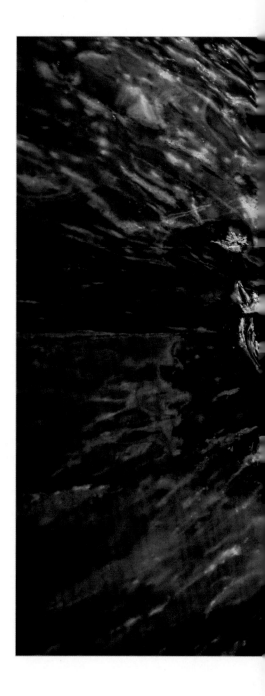

27
November

Success is not final, failure is not fatal:
it is the courage to continue that counts.

– Winston Churchill

28
November

Strive not to be a success,
but rather to be of value.

– Albert Einstein

29
November

I have always believed, and I still
believe, that whatever good or bad
fortune may come our way we can
always give it meaning and transform it
into something of value.

– Hermann Hesse

30
November

What you are will show
in what you do.

– Thomas A. Edison

1

December

Your work is going to fill a large part of your life,
and the only way to be truly satisfied is to do what you believe
is great work. And the only way to do great work is to love
what you do. If you haven't found it yet, keep looking. Don't settle.
As with all matters of the heart, you'll know when you find it.

– Steve Jobs

DECEMBER

2

December

Always do your best.
Your best is going to change from moment to moment;
it will be different when you are healthy as opposed
to sick. Under any circumstance, simply do your
best, and you will avoid self-judgment,
self-abuse and regret.

– Don Miguel Ruiz

3

December

After these two, Dr. Diet
and Dr. Quiet, Dr. Merriman
is requisite to preserve health.

– James Howell

4

December

I hated every minute of training,
but I said, "Don't quit. Suffer now and
live the rest of your life as a champion."

– Muhammad Ali

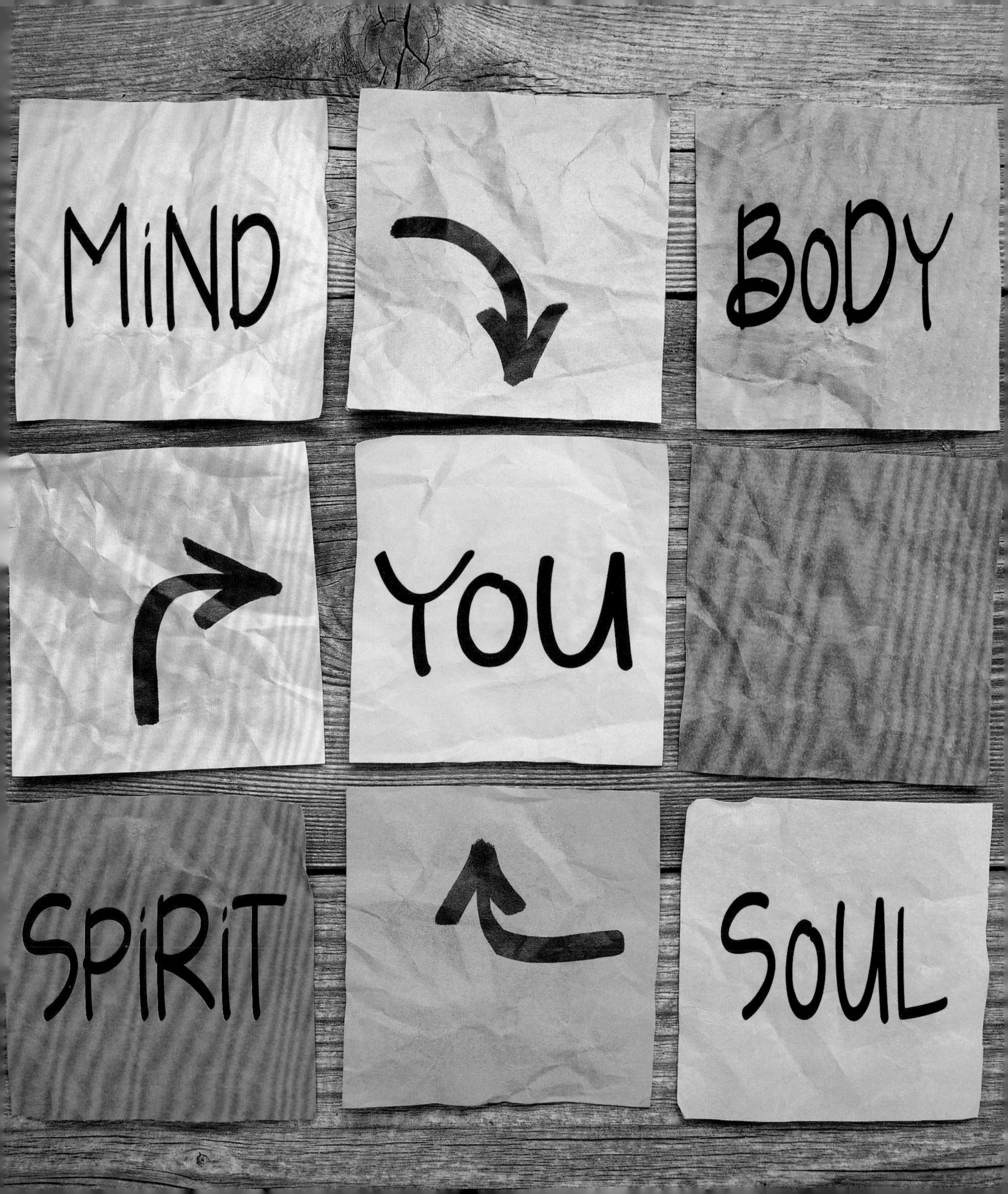
MiND
BODY
YOU
SPiRiT
SOUL

5

December

We all need people who will give us feedback.
That's how we improve.

– Bill Gates

6

December

Turn off your devices long before bed.
These devices emit light in the blue
spectrum, which disrupts sleep.
It shuts down production of the sleep-
enhancing hormone melatonin when it
hits your retina.

– Advice for your well-being

7

December

Sleep is a sort of innocence
and purification.

– Henri-Frédéric Amiel

8

December

One kind word can warm three winter months.

– Japanese proverb

9

December

Time and health are two precious assets
that we don't recognize and appreciate
until they have been depleted.

– *Denis Waitley*

10
December

The orange is a real cure-all for health and beauty. It is rich in the anti-oxidizing power of vitamin C, and combats free radicals and consequent aging.

– Advice for your well-being

11
December

Respect your body, fuel your body, challenge your body, move your body. And most of all, love your body.

– Advice for your well-being

12

December

Resist your fear; fear will never lead to
you a positive end. Go for your faith and
what you believe.

– T. D. Jakes

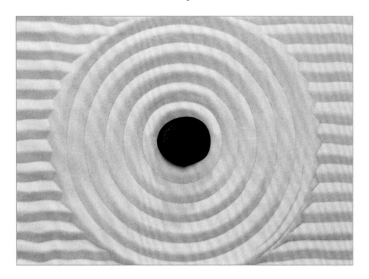

13

December

Success is nothing more than a few
simple disciplines, practiced every day.

– Jim Rohn

14

December

Half an hour's meditation each day is
essential, except when you are busy.
Then a full hour is needed.

– Saint Francis de Sales

15

December

The value of an idea lies
in the using of it.

– Thomas A. Edison

16

December

You will get there when you are meant to
get there and not one moment sooner...
so relax, breathe, and be patient.

– Mandy Hale

17

December

Steal all the colors of the world and paint
the canvas of your life by eliminating
the gray of the fears and anxieties.

– Omar Falworth

18
December

If you want something you've never had,
you must be willing to do something
you've never done.

– Thomas Jefferson

19
December

Courage is the first of human
qualities because it is the quality
which guarantees the others.

– Aristotle

20
December

Success depends upon previous preparation, and without such preparation there is sure to be failure.

– Confucius

21
December

I am not what happened to me,
I am what I choose to become.

– Carl Gustav Jung

22

December

The price of anything is the amount
of life you exchange for it.

– Henry David Thoreau

23

December

Those who are possessed by nothing
possess everything.

– Morihei Ueshiba

24

December

Thousands of candles can be lighted from
a single candle, and the life of the candle
will not be shortened. Happiness never
decreases by being shared.

– Buddha

25

December

Be content with what you have; rejoice
in the way things are. When you realize
there is nothing lacking, the whole
world belongs to you.

– Lao Tzu

26

December

It had long since come to my attention that people of accomplishment rarely sat back and let things happen to them. They went out and happened to things.

– *Leonardo da Vinci*

27

December

Excellence is an art won by training and
habituation. We do not act rightly because
we have virtue or excellence, but we rather
have those because we have acted rightly.
We are what we repeatedly do. Excellence,
then, is not an act but a habit.

– *Aristotle*

28

December

Belief comes spontaneously as well
as by effort. Belief is power.

– Sri Chinmoy

29

December

No amount of fire or freshness
can challenge what a man will store up
in his ghostly heart.

– F. Scott Fitzgerald

30

December

To face life, it is not enough to be capable, skilful, intelligent. One must also be courageous, tenacious, and succeed in controlling one's own anxiety and that of others.

— *Francesco Alberoni*

31

December

Determine never to be idle. No person will have occasion to complain of the want of time who never loses any. It is wonderful how much may be done if we are always doing.

— *Thomas Jefferson*

LIST OF CONTRIBUTORS

A

Aeschylus, 525-456 BC, Greek playwright (March 6)

Alberoni, Francesco, 1929-, Italian sociologist, journalist, and writer (December 30)

Allen, Woody (Heywood Allen), 1935-, American director, actor, and screenwriter (October 9)

Amiel, Herni-Frédéric, 1821-1881, Swiss philosopher and poet (December 7)

Angelou, Maya, 1928-2014, American poet, painter and dancer (January 30, March 2, July 4)

Aristotle, ca. 384-322 BC, Greek philosopher (March 19, April 22, June 23, June 30, July 26, August 5, October 20, December 19, December 27)

Augustine, Saint, 354-430, Latin philosopher and theologian (July 19)

Aurelius, Marcus Antoninus Augustus, 121-180, Roman emperor, philosopher and writer (September 12)

B

Bacon, Francis, 1561-1626, British philosopher, politician, and jurist (October 26)

Baden-Powell, Robert, 1857-1941, British soldier, educator, and writer (January 4)

Battaglia, Romano, 1933-2012, Italian journalist and author (September 29)

Baudelaire, Charles Pierre, 1821-1867, French poet (April 30)

Benjelloun, Abdelmajid, 1944-, Moroccan author and historian (March 26)

Bernard of Clairvaux, Saint, 1090-1153, French monk and abbot (August 29)

Billings, Josh, 1818-1885, American author (February 13)

Bonaparte, Napoleon, 1769-1821, French military and political leader (January 3)

Brazzi, Rossano (in the role of Charles Edouard de Valhubert), 1916-1994, Italian actor and film director (June 21)

Brown, Les (Leslie Calvin), 1946-, American motivational speaker (November 18)

Buddha, Siddhartha Gautama, 6th century BC, Founder of Buddhism (January 31, February 25, April 8, October 17, December 24)

Bukowski, Henry Charles, 1920-1994, American poet and writer (March 11)

Byron, Lord (George Gordon Noel Byron), 1788-1824, British poet and politician (September 16)

C

Camus, Albert, 1913-1960, French philosopher, writer, and playwright (September 27, October 7)

Cervantes, Miguel de, 1547-1616, Spanish writer and poet (April 12, June 10)

Chatwin, Bruce Charles, 1940-1998, British author (July 7)

Chopin, Fryderyk Franciszek, 1810-1849, Polish-born French composer and pianist (October 8)

Chopra, Deepak, 1946-, Indian physician (January 2, May 30, July 20)

Chu Hui Weng, 488-432 BC, Chinese King of the State of Chu (February 24)

Churchill, Winston, 1874-1965, British statesman (November 20, November 27)

Gates, Bill, 1955-, American founder and CEO of the Microsoft Corporation (February 22, May 14, August 27, December 5)

Gere, Richard, 1949-, American actor (August 18)

Gibran, Khalil, 1883-1931, Lebanese-American artist, poet, writer and philosopher (March 24, July 10)

Giono, Jean, 1895-1970, French author (September 3)

Goethe, Johann Wolfgang von, 1749-1832, German poet and writer (January 10, February 6, August 19, September 11, September 25)

Goldberg, Natalie, 1948-, American writer (August 6)

Guillemets, Terri, American quotation anthologist and writer (February 12, July 6)

H

Hale, Mandy, 1980-, British blogger and writer (December 16)

Hawking, Stephen William, 1942-, British physicist, mathematician, cosmologist, astrophysicist and writer (January 9, February 17, March 14, April 21, August 2, August 9, September 18)

Henepola Gunaratana, Bhante, 1927-, Sri Lankan Buddhist monk (March 4)

Heraclitus, 535-475 BC, Greek philosopher (March 15, November 11)

Hesse, Hermann, 1877-1962, German-born Swiss writer (May 4, November 29)

Hippocrates, 460-370 BC, Greek physician (June 14, August 22)

Hofmann, Hans, 1880-1966, German painter (May 26)

Howell, James, 1594-1666, Anglo-Welsh historian and writer (December 3)

Humboldt, Wilhelm von, 1767-1835, Prussian philosopher, diplomat, and founder of the Humboldt University of Berlin (January 5)

Hunt, James Henry Leigh, 1784-1859, British poet and writer (May 15)

I

Irving, John Winslow, 1942-, American author and screenwriter (September 13)

Iyengar, Bellur Krishnamachar Sundararaja "B.K.S.", 1918-2014, Indian founder of the style of yoga (January 8, August 31, October 16)

J

Jacques de Bourbon, 1870-1931, Duke of Madrid, claimant to the throne of Spain (October 5)

Jakes, Thomas Dexter "T. D.", 1957-, American pastor, writer and filmmaker (December 12)

James, William, 1842-1910, American psychologist and philosopher (September 23)

Jefferson, Thomas, 1743-1826, American politician, scientist and architect (December 18, December 31)

Jobs, Steve, 1955-2011, American entrepreneur and computer scientist (December 1)

John Paul II (Karol Józef Wojtya), 1920-2005, Catholic pope (March 10)

Jung, Carl Gustav, 1875-1961, Swiss psychiatrist and psychotherapist (January 21, January 27, September 21, December 21)

K

Kaye, Danny, (David Daniel Kaminsky), 1911-1987, American actor (May 27)

Kelsang Gyatso, Geshe, 1931-, Tibetan Buddhist monk (March 22)

Kennedy, John Fitzgerald, 1917-1963, Thirty-fifth President of the United States (May 31)

Kerouac, Jack, 1922-1969, American writer and poet (January 7)

Kierkegaard, Søren Aabye, 1813-1855, Danish philosopher

and theologian (January 15, March 18, April 3, June 7, August 12)

Kiyosaki, Robert, 1947-, American businessman and writer (October 25)

K. Pattabhi Jois, 1915-2009, Indian yoga teacher (July 27)

Krishnamurti, Jiddu, 1895-1986, Indian philosopherand writer (November 24)

Kurosawa, Akira, 1910-1998, Japanese film director, producer and author (October 4)

L

La Bruyère, Jean de, 1645-1696, French moralist and author (February 21)

Lagerfeld, Karl, 1933-, German stylist, photographer and film director (March 25)

Lao Tzu, VI century BC, Chinese philosopher (January 14, January 20, February 4, April 19, April 23, June 11, June 19, August 14, August 21, September 2, September 7, September 10, September 28, October 22, December 25)

Lee, Bruce Jun Fan, 1940-1973, Hong Kong American actor, martial arts instructor and filmmaker (February 5)

Leonardo da Vinci, 1452-1519, Italian painter, engineer and scientist (December 26)

Lewis, Clive Staples, 1898-1963, English writer and philologist (July 21)

Lewis, Ray Anthony, 1975-, former American football player (July 3)

Licalzi, Lorenzo, 1956-, Italian author (June 6)

Lincoln, Abraham, 1809-1865, Sixteenth President of the United States (October 2, November 12)

Littleword, Stephen, 1954-, American author (May 11, September 20)

Luther, Martin, 1483-1546, German theologian (October 13)

Lynch, David Keith, 1946-, American director, screenwriter, and producer (May 7)

M

MacFarlane, Linda, 1956-, American author (May 24)

MacLaine, Shirley, 1934, American actress (November 14)

Maharishi Mahesh Yogi, 1918-2008, Indian philosopher and guru (May 22, June 25, October 6)

Malaparte, Curzio (Kurt Erich Suckert), 1989-1957, Italian author and journalist (October 11)

Manroo, Tagor, Indonesian author (November 15)

Marcus Valerius Martial, 38/4– 102/104 A.D., Roman poet (November 2)

Marine, Joshua J., American author (April 26)

Marston, Ralph, 1955-, American writer (April 7)

Masson, Jeffrey Moussaieff, 1941-, American psychoanalyst and writer (August 16)

Maurois, André (Émile Salomon Wilhelm Herzog), 1885-1967, French writer (November 7)

McCarthy, Cormac, 1933-, American author and screenwriter (February 19)

McWilliams, Peter Alexander, 1949-2000, American author (October 1)

Merton, Thomas, 1915-1968, American writer and religious (November 10)

Miller, Henry, 1891-1980, American writer (April 6)

Monroe, Marilyn (Norma Jeane Mortenson), 1926-1962, American actress (June 9)

Montaigne, Michel, de, 1533-1592, French philosopher, writer and politician (March 30)

Montale, Eugenio, 1896-1981, Italian Nobel Prize Laureate in Literature, poet and author (March 27)

Schiaparelli, Elsa, 1890-1973,
Italian fashion designer
(July 1)

Schopenhauer, Arthur, 1788-
1860, German philosopher
(May 23)

Schwarzenegger, Arnold, 1947-,
Austrian-American actor and
politician (June 12)

Severgnini, Giuseppe, 1956-,
Italian journalist (July 2)

Shakespeare, William, 1564-
1616, British playwright and
poet (April 17, May 1, May 2)

Smiles, Samuel, 1812-1904,
Scottish author and reformer
(September 8)

Sogyal Rinpoche, 1947-,
Tibetan Buddhist master
(August 30)

Sophocles, 496-406 BC, Greek
playwright (April 20)

Sowell, Thomas, 1930-,
American economist and
writer (January 25)

Sri Chinmoy, 1931-2007, Indian
spiritual teacher (December 28)

Stanhope, Philip, 4th Earl of
Chesterfield, 1694-1773, British
noble and politician (June 1)

Steinbeck, John, 1902-1968,
American writer
(September 30)

Stevenson, Robert Louis Balfour,
1850-1894, Scottish writer
(September 4, September 26)

T

Tagore, Rabindranath, 1861-
1941, Bengali poet, writer
and essayist (March 1,
April 25)

Tamaro, Susanna, 1957-, Italian
writer (May 25)

Thales of Miletus, 624-546 BC,
Greek philosopher,
mathematician and
astronomer (July 9)

Theresa of Calcutta, Mother
(Anjëzë Gonxhe Bojaxhiu),
1910-1997, Albanian religious
(January 17, April 16)

Thich Nhat Hanh, 1926-,
Vietnamese Buddhist monk,
poet and activist (March 13,
March 16, June 24, October 18,
November 22)

Thoreau, Henry David,
1817-1862, American
philosopher, writer, and poet
(February 2, February 16,
April 24, May 9, June 16, July 5,
August 28, December 22)

Tolstoy, Leo Nikolayevich, 1828-
1910, Russian writer and
philosopher (January 23)

Tutu, Desmond Mpilo, 1931-,
South African clergyman and
activist (August 4)

Twain, Mark (Samuel
Langhorne Clemens), 1835-
1910, American writer (June 17,
October 10)

U

Ueshiba, Morihei, 1883-1969,
Japanese founder of
Aikido and martial artist
(April 5, April 13, May 10,
June 28, November 26,
December 23)

V

Verne, Jules, 1828-1905, French
writer (May 16)

Virgil, Maro Publius, 70-19 BC,
Roman poet (June 4)

Voltaire (François-Marie
Arouet), 1694-1778, French
writer and philosopher
(August 8)

W

Waitley, Denis, 1933-, American
writer (December 9)

Wilde, Oscar, 1854-1900, Irish
poet, writer, and playwright
(June 15)

Winfrey, Oprah, 1954-,
American anchorwoman
and actress (July 16)

Y

Ymber Delecto, American
author (July 29)

Yousafzai, Malala, 1997-,
Pakistani Nobel Peace Prize
Laureate, student and activist
(October 30)

PHOTO CREDITS

JULY

1, Jacek Nowak/123RF; 2, rido/123RF; 3, Ann Dudko/123RF; 4 and 5, Elena Elisseeva/123RF; 6, shironosov/Istockphoto; 7, shironosov/Istockphoto; 8 and 9, Alona Rjabceva/Istockphoto; 10, Liliia Rudchenko/123RF; 11, Komkrit Preechachanwate/123RF; 12 and 13, Mythja Photography/123RF; 14 and 15, Ls9907/Istockphoto; 16 and 17, Pedro Antonio SalaverrÃa Calahorra/123RF; 18 and 19, Roberto Atencia Gutierrez/123RF; 20 and 21, farang/123RF; 22, solarseven/123RF; 23, 24 and 25, Irina Belousa/123RF; 26, Mark Bridger/123RF - pat138241/123RF; 27 and 28, sjenner13/123RF; 29, sjenner13/123RF; 30 and 31, mediaphotos/Istockphoto.

AUGUST

1, Elena Schweitzer/123RF; 2 and 3, Dean Fikar/123RF; 4 and 5, haveseen/123RF; 6 and 7, mihtiander/123RF; 8 and 9, Mark Bridger/123RF; 10 and 11, Ersler Dmitry/123RF; 12 and 13, Liliia Rudchenko/123RF; 14, kritchanut/123RF; 15, aldorado10/123RF; 16 and 17, damedeeso/123RF; 18 and 19, Sujin Jetkasettakorn/123RF; 20, Anett Bakos/123RF; 21, Laurentiu Iordache/123RF; 22 and 23, Yulia Davidovich/123RF; 24, Anek Suwannaphoom/123RF; 25, khunaspix/123RF; 26 and 27, Icalek/123RF; 28 and 29, khunaspix/123RF; 30 and 31, Ann Dudko/123RF.

SEPTEMBER

1, Massimo De Candido/123RF; 2 and 3, lakhesis/123RF; 4 and 5, Eleni Seitanidou/123RF; 6 and 7, mettus/123RF; 8, Mythja Photography/123RF; 9, yelenayemchuk/123RF; 10 and 11, damedeeso/123RF; 12 and 13, FredFroese/Istockphoto; 14 and 15, tanjichica7/Istockphoto; 16 and 17, Andrew Rich/Istockphoto; 18 and 19, sval/123RF; 20 and 21, Olha Rohulya/123RF; 22 and 23, Polsin Junpangpen/123RF; 24 Laurin Rinder/123RF; 25 and 26, epicstockmedia/123RF; 27 and 28, pictureguy66/123RF; 29, Nina Vlassova/123RF; 30, Lane Erickson/123RF.

OCTOBER

1, Nina Vlassova/123RF; 2 and 3, Michael Lane/123RF; 4 and 5, damedeeso/123RF; 6 and 7, David Lee/123RF; 8, Darya Petrenko/123RF; 9, Darya Petrenko/123RF; 10, Ron Sumners/123RF; 11 and 12, Worradirek Muksab/123RF; 13 and 14, OksanaKiian/Istockphoto; 15, 16 and 17, Périg MORISSE/123RF; 18, yelenayemchuk/123RF; 19 and 20, Vladimir Salman/123RF; 21, Nina Vlassova/123RF; 22, Jaroslaw Grudzinski/123RF; 23 and 24, Anan Kaewkhammul/123RF; 25 and 26, ssilver/123RF; 27, 28 and 29 elwynn/123RF; 30 and 31, garloon/123RF.

NOVEMBER

1, Nina Vlassova/123RF; 2 and 3, Kontrec/Istockphoto; 4 and 5, Oleksandr Mudretsov/123RF; 6 and 7, Paul Grecaud/123RF; 8 and 9, elwynn/123RF; 10 and 11, Kenneth Keifer/123RF; 12, Mikel Martinez De Osaba/123RF; 13, Mikel Martinez De Osaba/123RF; 14 and 15, Richard Semik/123RF; 16 and 17, byheaven/Istockphoto; 18 and 19, PeopleImages/i Stock Photo; 20 and 21 Arturas Kerdokas/123RF; 22 and 23, zagart701/123RF; 24, Ratanaros Sarakut/123RF; 25 and 26, Johann Helgason/123RF; 27, Olha Rohulya/123RF; 28, Berangere Duforets/123RF; 29 and 30, Joerg Hachemann/123RF.

DECEMBER

1, elwynn/123RF; 2, Yanika Panfilova/123RF; 3 and 4, Marek Uliasz/123RF; 5, Aleksandr Ermolaev/123RF; 6 and 7, Aleksander Raths/123RF; 8 and 9, Alexandr Pakhnyushchyy/123RF; 10 and 11, Daria Zuykova/123RF; 12, Matt Trommer/123RF; 13, filmfoto/123RF; 14 and 15, lassedesignen/123RF; 16 and 17, 501room/123RF; 18, Aleksandr Makarenko/123RF; 19, Aleksandr Makarenko/123RF; 20 and 21, pljvv/123RF; 22, elen/123RF; 23, Shaiith/Istockphoto; 24 and 25, Chonlawit Boonprakob/123RF; 26 and 27, Steve Byland/123RF; 28, Lindsay Douglas/123RF; 29, Lindsay Douglas/123RF; 30 and 31, Alexey Stiop/123RF.

Project Editor
Valeria Manferto De Fabianis

Edited by
Laura Accomazzo

Graphic design
Paola Piacco

WHITE STAR PUBLISHERS

WS White Star Publishers® is a registered trademark
property of White Star s.r.l.

© 2016 White Star s.r.l.
Piazzale Luigi Cadorna, 6
20123 Milan, Italy
www.whitestar.it

Translation: Iceigeo, Milan (Jonathan West and Francesca Mottadelli)

ISBN 978-88-544-1065-7
2 3 4 5 6   23 22 21 20 19

Printed in China